BRIDGING MINDS

What AI Learns, What Humans Understand

By Beverly Simmons

Printing Futures

Printing Futures

Bridging Minds

ISBN-13: 978-1-942357-96-4

Paperback Version

Cover design by: Book Cover Illustrator

By jimtheaiwhisperer.com

Dedication

To my fellow educators—those I've taught beside, learned from, and shared the journey with.

I wrote Bridging Minds because today's students are growing up in a world profoundly shaped by artificial intelligence—and we, as educators, deserve professional development that reflects the urgency and complexity of that reality.

This book is dedicated to all of you who have always done your best to prepare students not just for the tests of today, but for the challenges of tomorrow.

TABLE OF CONTENTS

Prologue: The Philosopher Who Asked AI to Think Twice

Bridging Minds:

What AI Learns, What Humans Understand

Prologue: The Philosopher Who Asked AI to Think Twice

In a quiet corner of Denver, Colorado, on a summer day in 1932, a boy was born who would one day ask humanity's machines the ultimate question: "Do you really understand?" That boy, John Searle, grew up to become one of the most provocative voices in modern philosophy, challenging not only how we think about ourselves but also how we think about thinking itself.

By the late 20th century, the world was abuzz with visions of artificial intelligence—machines that could rival, and perhaps even surpass, human minds. But where others saw the glittering promise of silicon minds, Searle saw something more troubling: a fundamental misunderstanding of what it means to "understand."

Searle was no stranger to tough questions. His early work in speech act theory, inspired by J.L. Austin, dissected the way we perform actions with words. Promises, commands, declarations— all, he argued, were not mere sounds but acts that shaped the fabric of human life. His 1969 book, Speech Acts: An Essay in the Philosophy of Language[i], became a cornerstone for linguists and philosophers alike, a guide to how our words make worlds.

But it was in 1980 that Searle truly left his mark. He penned a paper titled Minds, Brains, and Programs[ii] and introduced the Chinese Room argument, a thought experiment that would ignite debates in classrooms, labs, and tech hubs for decades. Imagine, he said, a man locked in a room with a set of instructions—rules for manipulating Chinese symbols. The man doesn't understand Chinese; he's simply following syntactic rules. To an outsider, however, his responses might seem indistinguishable from those of a native speaker.

This, Searle argued, was the essence of artificial intelligence. A computer, like the man in the room, could shuffle symbols according to rules, but it could never truly understand them. It lacked the inner life—the subjective, conscious experience—that defines human minds. For Searle, this distinction wasn't a footnote; it was the foundation of his critique of "strong AI," the idea that machines could one day be conscious.

Philosophers, computer scientists, and AI enthusiasts were quick to push back. Couldn't the man in the room eventually learn to understand Chinese? Wasn't the room itself—the man and the instructions combined—a kind of mind? Yet, for all the counterarguments, Searle's thought experiment endured, a thorn in the side of anyone who dared to equate computation with comprehension.

Searle's intellectual pursuits didn't stop with AI. He ventured into the realm of social ontology, asking how human beings, through shared intentions and language, create the structures of society— money, governments, universities—that seem as real as the natural world. His 1995 book, The Construction of Social Reality, examined how collective agreement turns the abstract into the concrete, a fitting complement to his lifelong quest to understand how meaning arises.

As a scholar, Searle was unyielding, often controversial, and deeply committed to the idea that philosophy wasn't just an academic exercise but a tool for navigating the profound questions of human existence.

In this book, as we delve into the intersection of artificial intelligence and education, Searle's legacy serves as both a caution and an inspiration. His work reminds us that while AI may dazzle with its capabilities, educators have a unique responsibility: to teach not just how machines think, but how—and why— humans understand.

And as we ask ourselves what role AI should play in shaping the next generation, we would do well to remember the philosopher from Denver who once asked, "What does it truly mean to know?"

Chapter 1: The Godfather's Dilemna

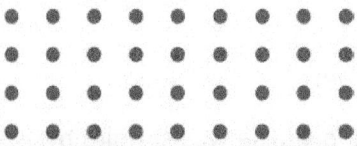

Chapter 1: The Godfather's Dilemma

In a small lecture hall in London in the mid-1960s, a young Geoffrey Hinton leaned forward in his seat, captivated by the discussion at hand. The topic was the brain—a labyrinth of neurons, each firing in an intricate dance that somehow gave rise to thought, emotion, and understanding. Hinton wasn't just interested in what the brain did; he wanted to understand how it did it.

This curiosity wasn't new. Growing up in London, Hinton had been the kind of child who disassembled clocks to see what made them tick. But now, as a student of experimental psychology, his focus had shifted to the ultimate puzzle: could the mechanics of the human mind be replicated in a machine?

Fast forward to the 1980s. The world of artificial intelligence was fragmented, caught between optimism and skepticism. While some researchers believed machines could one day match human intelligence, others scoffed at the idea. Hinton, by then a professor and researcher, was squarely in the camp of the dreamers. But he wasn't content with dreams—he wanted proof.

In those years, Hinton and his colleagues were refining an idea called the backpropagation algorithm. The premise was simple: by feeding data into a neural network and adjusting its parameters layer by layer, the network could learn from its mistakes. It was a method inspired by biology, mimicking the way neurons in the brain adapt and connect.

But not everyone was convinced. Neural networks were considered fringe science—too computationally expensive, too impractical for real-world applications. Funding was scarce, and skeptics were loud. Yet, Hinton pressed on, convinced that the key to replicating human cognition lay in these digital neurons.

By 2006, the tide was turning. Hinton and his team introduced Deep Belief Networks, demonstrating that their neural models could not only learn but also uncover patterns in vast amounts of data. Suddenly, the doubters were paying attention. The algorithms that had been dismissed as academic exercises were now solving problems that traditional methods couldn't touch.

And then came 2012, the year that cemented Hinton's legacy. He and his team developed a neural network capable of recognizing objects in YouTube videos with unprecedented accuracy. The breakthrough caught the attention of Google, which quickly brought Hinton on board. His work became the backbone of Google Brain, influencing everything from image search to voice recognition.

But for Hinton, the story didn't end with success. By the 2020s, as artificial intelligence surged ahead, he began to see the shadows cast by its brilliance. Machines could now write convincing essays, compose music, even diagnose diseases. Yet, this power came with risks: biased algorithms, potential job displacement, and the ominous question of whether AI might one day surpass human control. In 2023, Hinton stepped down from his role at Google, not to retire, but to sound the alarm. He warned that the unchecked development of AI could lead to unforeseen consequences, likening it to "an asteroid we're racing to understand before it hits." His message was clear: with great power comes great responsibility, and the tech world wasn't taking that responsibility seriously enough.

The following year, Hinton's career came full circle. In 2024, he was awarded the Nobel Prize in Physics—a historic recognition of his work on artificial neural networks. The announcement was met with both celebration and reflection. Here was a man who had not only pioneered the field of deep learning but had also become its most vocal critic.

As the lights dimmed in Stockholm's grand auditorium, Hinton stood at the podium, his words carrying the weight of decades of experience. "We've built something extraordinary," he said, "but extraordinary things demand extraordinary care. Let's make sure we're ready for what comes next." The applause was thunderous, but Hinton's mind was already elsewhere. He wasn't thinking about the accolades or the milestones. He was thinking about the future—a future shaped by algorithms and ethics, by progress and peril.

And in that moment, one thing as clear: Geoffrey Hinton wasn't just the godfather of AI; he was its conscience.

Today, he is evaluating that future with some regret for the role he has played in the development of AI. Hinton recently said, "You see, we've never had to deal with things more intelligent than ourselves before." He explained that during the industrial revolution, strength was no longer the guage of a valuable worker because if one wanted to dig a ditch, a machine could do that work more efficiently than a human. Some jobs were eliminated, but there was never any chance that those machines were going to become smarter than the humans who controlled them.

He continued, "How many examples do you know of a more intelligent thing being controlled by a less intelligent thing? There are very few examples. There's a mother and baby. Evolution put a lot of work into allowing the baby to control the mother, but that's about the only example I know of." He then described humans as toddlers when compared to advanced AI systems. "I like to think of it as: imagine yourself and a three-year-old. We'll be three-year-olds," he said [1].

Chapter 2: Introduction to AI and Philosophy

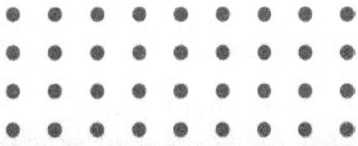

Chapter 2: Introduction to AI and Philosophy

The Rise of Artificial Intelligence

The rise of artificial intelligence (AI) marks a significant turning point in the way we understand both technology and human cognition. Over the past few decades, advancements in computational power, data analytics, and algorithmic design have propelled AI from theoretical discussions to practical applications in various fields, including education. Educators are now faced with the opportunity to integrate AI into their teaching methodologies, enhancing the learning experience while simultaneously grappling with the philosophical implications of these technologies. The exploration of AI's capabilities raises questions about intelligence, consciousness, and the fundamental nature of understanding, particularly through the lens of the Chinese Room argument.

The Chinese Room argument, proposed by philosopher John Searle, serves as a critical framework for assessing the limits of machine understanding. In this thought experiment, Searle illustrates that a person inside a room, following rules to manipulate Chinese symbols without any knowledge or understanding of the language, can produce coherent responses to questions posed in Chinese. This scenario challenges the notion that mere symbol manipulation equates to genuine understanding or consciousness. For educators, this raises essential questions about the role of AI in the classroom: Can machines genuinely comprehend the material they teach, or are they simply sophisticated tools that can simulate understanding without possessing it?

As AI technologies become increasingly integrated into educational practices, educators must reflect on the implications of the Chinese Room argument for machine learning. While AI can analyze data, personalize learning experiences (like recommending reading levels in Lexia or Khan Academy), and provide instant feedback, it lacks the teacher's ability to notice a student's confusion by facial expression or respond to a teachable moment. This absence of genuine comprehension means educators must remain central to the educational process. The relationship between human educators and AI tools should not be viewed as one of replacement but rather as a partnership, where the unique qualities of human cognition—empathy, contextual understanding, and ethical reasoning—are complemented by AI's capabilities for data processing and pattern recognition.

Furthermore, the debate surrounding the future of consciousness in relation to AI remains a rich area of inquiry. If machines can simulate human-like responses, what does this mean for our understanding of consciousness itself?

Are human-like responses sufficient for attributing consciousness, or must there be an intrinsic understanding? As educators navigate these philosophical waters, they can foster critical thinking and ethical considerations among students, equipping them to engage thoughtfully with emerging technologies.

The rise of artificial intelligence presents both opportunities and challenges for educators. By examining the implications of the Chinese Room argument and engaging with the broader philosophical questions surrounding AI, educators can better prepare themselves and their students for a future where technology and human cognition intersect. Integrating AI into educational settings should not be seen purely as a technological shift but rather as an invitation to explore more profound questions about understanding, intelligence, and what it means to be human in an increasingly automated world.

Overview of the Chinese Room Argument

The Chinese Room Argument, proposed by philosopher John Searle in 1980, is a thought experiment that challenges the notion of understanding in artificial intelligence. The argument presents a scenario in which a person who does not speak Chinese is placed inside a room with a set of rules for manipulating Chinese symbols. This person can respond to Chinese characters slipped under the door by producing appropriate responses based solely on these rules, without any understanding of the language itself. Searle uses this scenario to argue that while a machine may appear to understand language through its outputs, it does not possess genuine understanding or consciousness.

In the context of AI, the Chinese Room raises critical questions about the capabilities and limitations of machine learning systems. While AI can process and generate human-like responses based on large datasets, the argument suggests that this does not equate to true comprehension or awareness. Educators— especially in subjects like language arts or social studies—might ask: If a chatbot generates a decent student essay, does that mean it 'understands' the Civil War? The Chinese Room suggests otherwise—it highlights how AI mimics understanding but lacks meaning-making, a skill we must still teach, especially as AI advances and integrates into educational environments.

The implications of the Chinese Room Argument extend to how we approach AI in educational settings. As educators increasingly incorporate AI tools into their curricula, it is essential to recognize that these systems operate without genuine understanding. This realization can influence how educators design learning experiences that leverage AI while fostering critical thinking about the nature of human and artificial intelligence. By discussing the nuances of the Chinese Room, educators can better equip students to engage with AI technologies thoughtfully and responsibly.

Moreover, the debate surrounding the Chinese Room raises important considerations about the future of consciousness and the philosophical underpinnings of AI. If machines can simulate human-like responses, what does this mean for our understanding of consciousness and self-awareness? Educators are uniquely positioned to facilitate discussions about these topics, encouraging students to explore the implications of AI on our conception of mind and existence. Engaging with the Chinese Room Argument can help demystify the complexities of AI and consciousness, fostering a deeper understanding of both.

Ultimately, the Chinese Room Argument serves as a crucial lens through which educators can examine the intersection of AI, philosophy, and pedagogy. By integrating discussions of this argument into their teaching, educators can inspire critical inquiry into the nature of intelligence, the capabilities of AI, and the ethical considerations surrounding its use. As we navigate an increasingly AI-driven world, the insights gained from the Chinese Room debate will be vital in shaping informed, conscientious citizens who can engage thoughtfully with technology.

Importance of Philosophy for Educators

The importance of philosophy for educators, particularly in the context of artificial intelligence, cannot be overstated. Philosophy provides a foundational framework for understanding complex concepts such as consciousness, cognition, and the implications of advanced technologies. For educators interested in AI, engaging with philosophical questions enables a deeper comprehension of what it means for machines to "understand" and interact with the world. Searle's Chinese Room argument serves as a critical lens through which educators can examine the limitations of machine learning and the nature of human-like understanding. By integrating philosophical inquiry into their teaching practices, educators can foster a more nuanced discussion around the capabilities and limitations of AI.

Educators equipped with philosophical insights can better navigate the ethical implications of AI in education. As AI systems become increasingly prevalent, questions surrounding bias, accountability, and the role of human oversight become paramount. Philosophy encourages educators to critically analyze these issues, promoting a more responsible approach to technology integration. Educators can create a more inclusive and equitable educational environment by questioning the assumptions underlying AI systems and their potential impact on learners. This reflective practice enhances their teaching strategies and prepares students to engage thoughtfully with the technologies that shape their lives.

The philosophy of mind plays a crucial role in shaping our understanding of AI interaction. Educators can employ philosophical concepts to explore the relationship between human cognition and machine processing. Educators can draw parallels between human learners and AI systems by examining theories that address the nature of thought and consciousness. This comparative analysis can illuminate discussions about the potential for AI to replicate human-like understanding or the limitations inherent in computational approaches. Such philosophical exploration can enrich the learning experience, encouraging students to assess the nature of intelligence critically.

Moreover, the implications of the Chinese Room argument for machine learning are particularly relevant for educators. This thought experiment challenges the notion that syntactic processing alone can lead to genuine understanding. By engaging with this argument, educators can stimulate discussions about the role of semantics in learning and knowledge acquisition. This inquiry can lead to a more profound appreciation of the complexities of human learning processes and the recognition that current AI technologies, despite their sophistication, may still lack the depth of understanding characteristic of human beings. Encouraging students to grapple with these philosophical dilemmas can foster critical thinking and a more profound grasp of AI's capabilities.

Finally, as we look to the future of consciousness in the context of AI, the philosophical discourse surrounding the Chinese Room debate becomes increasingly vital. Understanding the potential trajectories of AI development requires an intellectual and philosophical lens that examines the essence of consciousness and self-awareness. Educators can play a pivotal role in guiding students[1] through these debates, helping them consider the broader implications of AI advancements on society and individual identity. By championing philosophical inquiry, educators deepen their understanding and empower students to engage with the profound questions that will define the future of AI and consciousness.

From Theory to Practice —

Making AI Philosophy Useful in Classrooms

This resource translates the philosophical ideas in Chapter 2—especially the Chinese Room argument—into practical classroom conversations, activities, and reflective tools for educators. It can also be used to guide department discussions or student-teacher seminars.

Try It: Sample Activities

1. Chinese Room Simulation

- One participant receives a rulebook to respond to phrases written in an unfamiliar language.
- Others pose questions in that language.
- The group reflects: Did the responder understand? Did they "think"?
- Use this to spark conversation about whether current AI tools "understand" or simply "respond."

2. Human or AI?

- Create a quiz using two responses to each question—one from AI and one from a student.
- Let participants guess the source, then reflect on why they chose what they did.
- What does it mean if AI can sound human? What's missing?

3. Would You Rather... (AI Edition)

- Would you rather learn math from an AI or a person?

- Would you trust AI to recommend books? To grade your essay?

- Encourage debate, emphasizing empathy, intent, and understanding.

👤 Philosophy Quick Hits (For Use in Class or PD)

Philosopher	What They Said	Classroom Tie-In
Alan Turing	"If a machine fools you, does it think?"	Use to discuss the Turing Test and simulations.
René Descartes	"I think, therefore I am."	Can AI say the same? What role does self-awareness play in learning?
Wittgenstein	"Meaning is use."	Does AI use language with intent or just form?
Nick Bostrom	"We must plan for AI's risks."	Frame questions of ethics and responsibility

✍️ Reflection Prompt

"Can something understand you if it can't feel or experience the world like you do?"

Use this in writing journals, exit slips, or group reflections.

Chapter 3: Understanding the Chinese Room

Chapter 3: Understanding the Chinese Room

Origin of the Chinese Room Thought Experiment

The Chinese Room thought experiment, introduced by philosopher John Searle in 1980, serves as a pivotal point of discussion in the philosophy of mind and artificial intelligence. Searle's aim was to challenge the prevailing notion of strong AI, which asserts that a computer running a program can possess a mind, consciousness, and understanding.

By presenting a scenario where a person inside a room manipulates Chinese symbols without understanding their meaning, Searle sought to illustrate that syntactic manipulation of symbols does not equate to semantic understanding. This thought experiment compels educators to reconsider the implications of machine learning systems and their capability to genuinely understand language versus merely processing it.

Searle's thought experiment was inspired by the philosophical debates surrounding the nature of cognition and understanding. Before introducing the Chinese Room, the Turing Test was the predominant measure of machine intelligence, proposing that if a machine could effectively imitate human conversation, it could be considered intelligent. Searle's argument, however, highlighted a crucial distinction between simulating understanding and actual comprehension. By placing a human operator in a controlled environment, Searle illustrated that even if the operator could produce appropriate responses in Chinese, they lacked any real understanding of the language. This distinction is fundamental for educators exploring the boundaries of AI capabilities and limitations.

The implications of the Chinese Room argument extend into various fields, particularly in machine learning and cognitive science. As AI systems become increasingly sophisticated, educators must grapple with whether these systems can truly understand the information they process or are merely executing programmed tasks. This inquiry leads to discussions about the nature of intelligence itself, prompting educators to teach students about the philosophical foundations underpinning AI technologies' development. By examining these distinctions, educators can better prepare students to engage critically with AI, understanding its capabilities and recognizing its limitations.

The Chinese Room thought experiment also raises questions about the future of consciousness concerning AI. If a machine can convincingly simulate human-like responses without genuine understanding, what does that mean for our conception of consciousness? Educators are tasked with exploring these profound questions, encouraging students to think deeply about the nature of mind and intelligence. As AI continues to evolve, the distinction between programmed responses and authentic understanding will remain a central topic of discussion in classrooms, influencing how future generations perceive and interact with intelligent systems.

The origin of the Chinese Room thought experiment is rooted in a critical examination of AI's potential and its limitations. By navigating the philosophical implications of Searle's argument, educators can foster a more nuanced understanding of the relationship between AI and human cognition. This exploration enhances the educational experience and equips students with the tools they need to engage thoughtfully with the rapidly advancing field of artificial intelligence. As discussions around the Chinese Room continue to unfold, they will undoubtedly shape the future of AI education and ethical considerations regarding machine consciousness.

Key Components of the Chinese Room

At its core, the Chinese Room illustrates a scenario in which an individual, who does not understand Chinese, is placed inside a room with a set of rules for manipulating Chinese symbols. This person can respond to Chinese queries by following these rules, thereby giving the appearance of understanding the language, even though actual comprehension is absent. The key components of this analogy highlight the distinction between syntax (structure) and semantics (meaning)—a bit like a student copying math formulas correctly without understanding what the variables represent. Mere symbol manipulation does not equate to true understanding or consciousness.

One of the crucial components of the Chinese Room is the distinction between "input" and "output." The input represents the questions or symbols presented to the individual inside the room, while the output signifies the responses generated based on the manipulation of these symbols. This separation is vital for educators to grasp, as it parallels the operations of AI systems, which process data inputs to produce outputs without genuine comprehension.

Another significant element is the role of the rulebook, which provides the instructions for manipulating symbols. This rulebook symbolizes the algorithms and programming that govern AI behavior. In the case of machine learning, algorithms can adapt and improve their performance through training on vast datasets. However, the Chinese Room argument posits that no matter how sophisticated the rulebook becomes, it cannot lead to true understanding or consciousness.

The observer's perspective also plays a key role in the Chinese Room argument. From the outside, the individual in the room appears to understand Chinese, much like a chatbot might 'sound' like it knows the answer to a historical question. But does it understand history, or is it just rearranging fact, leading observers to mistakenly attribute understanding to the system as a whole. This raises important questions about how we judge intelligence and comprehension in AI, prompting educators to reflect on the criteria used to evaluate AI systems.

Lastly, the implications of the Chinese Room for the future of consciousness and AI are significant. The argument suggests that machines, regardless of their sophistication, may never achieve true consciousness or understanding. This raises questions about the nature of consciousness itself and whether it is a uniquely human attribute. By dissecting the components of the Chinese Room, educators can equip students with the tools to critically analyze AI technologies and their impact on human thought and understanding.

Implications for Understanding AI

The implications of understanding artificial intelligence through the lens of the Chinese Room argument are profound for educators. The Chinese Room challenges the notion that mere syntactic manipulation of symbols can lead to genuine understanding or consciousness. For educators, this raises critical questions about how AI systems, which often operate on similar principles, can be integrated into educational frameworks. It invites a deeper examination of what it means to understand content, engage with knowledge, and communicate effectively in an age increasingly dominated by intelligent systems.

Educators are encouraged to explore the distinction between human cognition and artificial processes in the context of the philosophy of mind. By recognizing the limitations of AI, educators can better navigate the integration of these tools in classrooms, ensuring that they enhance rather than replace human interaction and critical thinking.

The implications for machine learning are equally significant. As AI technologies evolve, the Chinese Room argument serves as a cautionary tale against overestimating the capabilities of machine learning systems. Understanding that these systems can simulate understanding without possessing it encourages a more nuanced approach to using AI in educational settings, prompting discussions on ethical considerations, potential biases in AI algorithms, and the importance of fostering authentic learning experiences among students.

Furthermore, the debate surrounding the future of consciousness in the context of AI and the Chinese Room opens up rich avenues for inquiry in the classroom. Educators can engage students in discussions about the nature of consciousness, the philosophical implications of AI, and the ethical dimensions of creating machines that might mimic human behavior. Encouraging students to think critically about these issues prepares them for a future where AI plays an increasingly prominent role in society, fostering a generation that is both technologically savvy and philosophically informed.

Ultimately, understanding AI through the framework of the Chinese Room argument equips educators with the tools to critically evaluate the role of AI in education. By fostering an environment where philosophical inquiry meets practical application, educators can help students navigate the complexities of an AI-driven world. This approach not only enriches the educational experience but also prepares students to engage thoughtfully with the ethical and philosophical challenges posed by artificial intelligence as it continues to evolve.

From Theory to Practice:

From Simulation to Meaning —
Project-Based Learning with the Chinese Room

This handout supports Chapter 3 of 'Bridging Minds' by translating the Chinese Room thought experiment into an experiential, project-based format that can be used with students or modeled in teacher training workshops. Participants will explore the limitations of AI systems by simulating how syntactic rule-following differs from true understanding.

Project Title: "Inside the Room: Can Machines Think?"

Objective: Students will simulate an AI system, explore the difference between understanding and output, and analyze the implications of the Chinese Room argument.

Part 1: The Simulation

Setup:

Create a message-passing station where one student (or group) follows a strict rulebook (created by the teacher) to answer questions written in symbolic form.

Use emojis, symbols, or a real language the responder doesn't understand.

Assign other students as message senders and observers.

Discussion Prompt:

- Did the "AI" understand the question or just follow steps?

- How does this relate to digital assistants like Siri, Alexa, or ChatGPT?

Part 2: Reverse Engineering the Rulebook

Have students write their own "rulebooks" that simulate answering yes/no questions or performing tasks without knowing the content.

Challenge them: How far can your rule-following system go before it *seems* intelligent?

Share examples and test their effectiveness.

Part 3: Ethics & Insight

Let students imagine roles that AI might fill in the future: teacher, judge, coach, principal.

 In groups, create short skits or video presentations exploring scenarios like:

  - An AI tutor that gives misleading feedback

  - A robot principal enforcing discipline

Discuss ethical boundaries and the human qualities missing from each system.

Final ReflectionPrompt students to write:

"Can something that never experiences joy, confusion, or motivation truly understand your needs as a learner?"

Chapter 4: Mind, Machines, and Meaning —
What AI Can't Teach Us About Learning

Chapter 4: Mind, Machines, and Meaning —

What AI Can't Teach Us About Learning

Your students don't just memorize content—they reshape it, apply it, and make it their own. Can machines do that?

In the vast landscape of educational psychology and cognitive science, we've come to understand that the human mind is far more than just a repository of information. Unlike a computer that simply stores and retrieves data, the human mind actively constructs meaning from experiences, interactions, and observations. This fundamental difference becomes increasingly relevant as we navigate the intersection of human learning and artificial intelligence in education.

The Constructive Nature of Human Learning

When we learn, we don't simply absorb information like a sponge. Instead, our minds actively engage in a complex process of meaning-making. Consider how a child learns about gravity - not through memorizing Newton's laws, but through countless experiences of dropping objects, falling down, and observing the world around them. This process of constructing understanding through experience forms the cornerstone of Jean Piaget's constructivist theory.

Piaget demonstrated that learning occurs through a dynamic interplay between assimilation (fitting new experiences into existing mental frameworks) and accommodation (adjusting those frameworks when new experiences don't fit). This process is inherently personal and often messy, involving trial and error, misconceptions, and gradual refinement of understanding.

The Social Dimension of Learning

Lev Vygotsky expanded our understanding by emphasizing the crucial role of social interaction in learning. His theory suggests that learning is fundamentally a social process, mediated through language, culture, and interaction with others. The concept of the "Zone of Proximal Development" - the gap between what a learner can do independently and what they can achieve with guidance - highlights how human learning thrives through collaboration and mentorship.

This social aspect of learning creates a rich tapestry of shared meaning and understanding that goes far beyond simple information transfer. When students discuss ideas, challenge each other's assumptions, and work together to solve problems, they're engaging in a uniquely human form of learning that AI, despite its capabilities, cannot fully replicate.

Beyond Memory: The Complexity of Understanding

Benjamin Bloom's taxonomy of learning objectives provides a crucial framework for understanding the depth and complexity of human learning. While lower-order thinking skills like remembering and understanding are important, human learning truly flourishes in the realm of higher-order thinking - analyzing, evaluating, and creating. These complex cognitive processes involve not just knowing facts, but being able to see connections, identify patterns, and generate new insights.

The Emotional Foundation of Learning

Perhaps one of the most significant distinctions between human learning and AI processing is the role of emotions. Human learning is deeply intertwined with emotional experiences. Fear, excitement, curiosity, and satisfaction all play crucial roles in how we learn and what we remember. A student's emotional state can either enhance or inhibit their learning, making the emotional aspect of education impossible to separate from the cognitive.

Context and Meaning in Human Learning

Humans don't learn in a vacuum. Every piece of information we encounter is filtered through our personal experiences, cultural background, and existing knowledge. This contextual nature of learning means that the same information can hold different meanings for different learners, leading to rich and diverse interpretations that enhance our collective understanding.

Implications for Education

Understanding these fundamental aspects of human learning has profound implications for education. While AI can be a powerful tool for supporting learning, it's essential to remember that human learning involves much more than processing information. It requires:

- Creating opportunities for active construction of knowledge
- Facilitating meaningful social interactions
- Engaging emotions and personal connections
- Supporting higher-order thinking skills
- Recognizing and valuing individual perspectives and experiences

As educators, our role is to create environments that support this complex, multifaceted process of human learning. While AI can assist in this endeavor, it cannot replace the uniquely human aspects of learning that make education such a transformative experience.

The challenge for modern educators is to harness the power of technology while preserving and enhancing the distinctly human elements of learning that make education meaningful and effective. By understanding how humans learn - through construction, social interaction, emotional engagement, and personal meaning-making - we can better serve our students in an increasingly technological world.

Can AI Learn Like a Student?

Machine learning (ML) differs fundamentally from human learning. ML models identify statistical patterns from massive datasets and use those to predict or generate outputs. In contrast, human learning is messy, contextual, and rooted in meaning-making. Students learn through trial, failure, questioning, and connecting new information to prior experiences.

Can AI Teach like a Classroom Educator?

AI can assist. It can simulate. But it cannot teach in the truest sense of the word.

Artificial intelligence doesn't learn, reflect, or understand as humans do. Instead, it processes vast amounts of data using algorithms that mimic human responses—producing patterns that feel intelligent but lack intention or awareness.

For educators, this difference isn't just technical—it's foundational.

When we bring AI tools like chatbots or writing assistants into the classroom, we're introducing systems that can replicate surface-level tasks but not deep learning. These tools don't "think." They don't question. They don't connect ideas with purpose or emotion.

This distinction is critical to teaching. Students need to know that while AI can offer useful suggestions, it lacks empathy, context, and the critical capacity to reason ethically or emotionally. It can mimic conversation—but not care. It can structure an argument—but not stand behind its beliefs.

From Chatbots to Deepfakes: The Rise of Digital Simulation

The ability of AI to simulate communication has grown rapidly—from casual chatbots to sophisticated deepfakes. These tools raise important questions about truth, authorship, and identity. For educators, they present both opportunity and risk.

- o   While AI can be a tool for creativity and productivity, it can also:
- o   Allow students to complete assignments without real understanding
- o   Blur the lines between authentic and artificial sources

o   Spread misinformation or deceptive media quickly

Our job isn't to eliminate these technologies—it's to equip students with the skills to question them.

Teaching Students to Think Beyond the Simulation

When AI can write, explain, or summarize, how do we protect learning? The answer lies in helping students develop intellectual resilience and ethical awareness—not just digital skills.

Three Core Areas for Educator Focus:

1. Academic Integrity

   o   Design tasks that require voice, originality, and application—not just facts.
   o   Ask for reflections, process notes, or annotated revisions to show thought behind answers.

Teach students how (and when) to cite AI support transparently.

2. Privacy & Protection

   o   Always vet AI platforms for data safety.
   o   Prefer district-approved tools.
   o   Help students understand how their data, writing, and voice can be collected or mimicked.

3. Digital Literacy & Citizenship

   o   Teach students to recognize AI-generated content.
   o   Explore questions of authorship, authenticity, and intent.

Frame AI not just as a tech tool, but as a civic and ethical issue.

Looking Ahead: What AI Can't Teach

AI will become more powerful. But that doesn't mean it will become more human. The future of education lies in what AI can't do:

- Feel wonder
- Ask original questions
- Build understanding through failure and experience
- Connect hearts and minds through shared learning
- As educators, our mission is not to compete with AI, but to develop the human capacities it cannot replicate.

Educators can move beyond discussion by engaging students in a hands-on simulation of the Chinese Room that grows into a full project. This allows learners to *experience* the central ideas of the thought experiment and reflect on AI's limits.

Project Title: "Inside the Room: Can Machines Think?"

Objective: Students will simulate an AI system, explore the difference between understanding and output, and analyze the implications of the Chinese Room argument.

Part 1: The Simulation

Setup:

- Create a *message-passing station* where one student (or group) follows a strict rulebook (created by the teacher) to answer questions written in symbolic form (could be emojis, symbols, or a real language the student doesn't understand).
- Other students act as observers or message senders.

Discussion Prompt:

- Did the "AI" understand the question or just follow steps?
- How does this relate to Siri, Alexa, or ChatGPT?

Part 2: Reverse Engineering the Rulebook

- Have students write their own "rulebooks" to simulate how they might answer yes/no questions or complete simple tasks *without understanding.*
- Then ask: How complex can your system get before it *seems* intelligent?

Part 3: Ethics & Insight

- Ask students to imagine a world where these "rule-following" machines decide grades, drive cars, or write laws.
- Let groups present brief skits or videos based on scenarios like:
  - An AI tutor giving incorrect feedback.
  - A school principal replaced by a robot.

Final Reflection

Prompt students to write:

"Can something that never experiences joy, confusion, or motivation truly understand your needs as a learner?"

Chapter 5: Implications of the Chinese Room Argument for Machine Learning

Chapter 5: Implications of the Chinese Room Argument for Machine Learning

Limitations of Current AI Systems

The limitations of current AI systems are multifaceted and deeply intertwined with philosophical inquiries surrounding consciousness and understanding, particularly in the context of the Chinese Room argument. One significant limitation, as discussed earlier, is the lack of true understanding or comprehension in AI systems. While they can process and analyze vast amounts of data, they do so without any awareness or intent. This raises critical questions about the nature of intelligence and whether the ability to perform tasks or generate responses equates to genuine understanding. Educators must grapple with these philosophical implications when integrating AI into educational settings, as it challenges traditional notions of learning and knowledge acquisition.

Another limitation is the dependency on data quality and quantity, which directly affects the performance and reliability of AI systems. Current AI models require large datasets to function effectively, and the biases present in these datasets can lead to skewed outcomes. This reliance on data not only highlights the shortcomings in AI's ability to generalize knowledge but also underscores the moral responsibility educators hold in selecting and curating the data used for training these systems. It is crucial for educators to be aware of these biases as they implement AI in classrooms, ensuring that AI tools promote equity and fairness in educational opportunities.

The interpretability of AI systems also presents a significant challenge. Many current AI models, particularly those based on deep learning, operate as "black boxes," making it difficult for educators to understand how decisions are made or to trace the rationale behind specific outputs. This lack of transparency can hinder trust in AI technologies and complicates their integration into educational practices. Educators must advocate for more interpretable models and seek ways to demystify AI processes for both themselves and their students, fostering a more informed approach to AI utilization in the learning environment.

Moreover, the limitations of current AI systems extend to their inability to engage in authentic dialogue or exhibit emotional intelligence. While chatbots and virtual assistants can mimic conversation and respond to queries, they lack the capacity for empathy, creativity, and emotional nuance that characterize human interactions.

This deficiency poses challenges in educational contexts where social and emotional learning are paramount. Educators are grappling with their need to add the human element that is essential for fostering genuine relationships and understanding in the classroom.

Lastly, the philosophical implications of the Chinese Room argument resonate with the limitations of current AI systems, particularly concerning the future of consciousness and machine learning. The argument posits that a system can manipulate symbols without any comprehension of their meaning, which reflects the operational nature of present-day AI. As educators explore the potential of AI in education, they must critically assess the boundaries of what these systems can achieve. The challenge lies not only in advancing AI technology but also in understanding its limitations, ensuring that as we bridge the gap between human cognition and machine processing, we maintain an awareness of the profound philosophical questions surrounding consciousness and the essence of understanding.

The Role of Syntax and Semantics

The relationship between syntax and semantics is fundamental to understanding both language and artificial intelligence. Syntax refers to the structure of language—how words are arranged to form sentences—while semantics deals with meaning. In the context of the Chinese Room argument, introduced by philosopher John Searle, the distinction between syntax and semantics becomes crucial. Searle posits that a machine following syntactical rules to manipulate symbols does not understand the meanings of those symbols. This raises important questions about whether AI can truly grasp language or simply simulate understanding through programmed responses.

In educational settings, recognizing the difference between syntax and semantics can help educators better understand the limitations of AI in language processing. When AI systems are designed to generate or interpret human language, they often rely on vast databases of syntactical structures and statistical correlations rather than a genuine comprehension of meaning. This distinction is pivotal for educators who aim to integrate AI tools into their curricula, as it highlights the need for critical thinking about the capabilities and shortcomings of these technologies. Such awareness can guide educators in fostering a more nuanced understanding of AI among students, encouraging them to question the nature of intelligence itself.

The implications of the Chinese Room argument for machine learning are profound. As machine learning algorithms become increasingly sophisticated, they often blur the lines between true understanding and mere mimicry. Educators must engage with these implications to prepare students for a future where AI systems are pervasive in various domains. By examining case studies of AI applications that excel in syntactical processing yet falter in semantic comprehension, educators can, as earlier examined, facilitate discussions about the philosophical underpinnings of these technologies. This encourages students to reflect on what it means for a machine to "know" something and how this relates to human cognition.

Furthermore, the debate surrounding consciousness in AI, particularly in relation to the Chinese Room, invites educators to ponder the future of intelligence itself. If machines can achieve high levels of syntactical processing but lack semantic understanding, what does this imply for the development of conscious AI? Educators can leverage this discourse to explore the ethical implications of creating machines that may one day exhibit behaviors indistinguishable from human responses, prompting discussions on the moral responsibilities that accompany such advancements. This exploration can enrich students' appreciation of the philosophical dimensions of AI, inspiring them to consider the broader societal impacts of their work.

Understanding the role of syntax and semantics in the context of AI and the Chinese Room argument offers valuable insights for educators. By understanding the limitations of AI in grasping meaning, educators can better prepare students to navigate a future where artificial intelligence is an integral part of their lives. Engaging with these philosophical questions not only enhances critical thinking but also fosters a deeper understanding of the potential and pitfalls of AI technologies. As educational institutions continue to incorporate AI into their frameworks, the discussion around syntax, semantics, and their implications will remain a vital component of preparing the next generation for a world increasingly shaped by intelligent machines.

Ethical Considerations in AI Development

The development of artificial intelligence (AI) raises significant ethical considerations that educators must understand to navigate the complexities of integrating AI into educational environments. One of the primary concerns revolves around the implications of the Chinese Room argument, which questions whether machines can truly understand or possess consciousness. This philosophical debate is crucial for educators as they consider the role of AI in teaching and learning. Educators must critically assess how AI systems might influence cognitive development, creativity, and the nature of understanding itself in students.

Another ethical consideration involves data privacy and the use of student information in AI systems. As AI applications become more prevalent in educational settings, they often rely on vast amounts of data to function effectively. Educators must grapple with the ethical implications of collecting and analyzing this data. Ensuring that student information is handled responsibly, securely, and transparently is paramount. This not only protects students' privacy but also fosters trust in the educational institution's use of AI technologies. Educators should advocate for policies that prioritize ethical data use while also educating students about their digital footprints.

The potential for bias in AI algorithms is another critical ethical issue. AI systems can inadvertently perpetuate existing biases if they are trained on datasets that reflect historical inequalities. This can lead to unfair treatment of students based on race, gender, or socio-economic status. Educators must be aware of these biases and actively work to mitigate them in the deployment of AI tools. This includes advocating for diverse datasets, ongoing bias detection, and promoting equity in AI applications. By prioritizing fairness, educators can help shape a future where AI technologies contribute positively to diverse learning communities.

Moreover, the integration of AI into education raises questions about the role of educators themselves. As AI systems become more capable of providing personalized learning experiences, there is concern about the diminishing role of teachers in the classroom. Educators need to reflect on how AI can complement their teaching rather than replace it. Maintaining a human element in education is essential for fostering critical thinking, emotional intelligence, and interpersonal skills. By emphasizing the importance of the teacher-student relationship, educators can ensure that AI serves as a tool for enhancement rather than a substitute for human interaction.

Finally, the ethical implications of AI development extend to the broader societal context in which education operates. As AI technologies evolve, educators must consider the potential long-term effects on societal values, employment, and the nature of consciousness itself. Engaging students in discussions about these ethical dilemmas can foster critical thinking and prepare them for a future where AI plays an integral role in various aspects of life.

By instilling a strong ethical framework in their teaching, educators can empower students to navigate the complexities of AI and contribute to a society that values responsible innovation.

The following fictionalized scenarios are meant to spark reflection and discussion. Educators are encouraged to treat them as exercises in strategic foresight—just like businesses or government agencies use simulations to anticipate unintended consequences in new technologies. These aren't real stories, but they're real *possibilities*.

This approach was modeled for me by someone I greatly admire: Tandi Begian, a NASA astronaut trainer whose husband was an astronaut. Tandi served on the board of the NEW Detroit Science Center, where I had the pleasure of working with her to develop exhibits that merged science, engineering, and imagination. Tandi once explained her role at NASA using two powerful examples. The first: 'You're sitting in a room and hear a 'clop clop clop' sound in the hallway. You assume it's a horse running past. But what if it's a child wearing his dad's snorkeling flippers?' Her job was to imagine the *unexpected explanation*, the flaw in our assumptions, and prepare astronauts to deal with it.

The second example she gave was far more physical. In the Science Center, we had proudly designed a hovercraft experience with a perfectly flat floor—a fun ride for families to glide on a cushion of air. Tandi, always thinking about edge cases, warned us: 'I can make someone sick in 30 seconds.' She had a staff member close his eyes, then gently shifted the hovercraft side to side in a slow, deliberate pattern she had used at NASA. Sure enough, the person was dizzy and nauseated within moments. Because of her insight, we were able to prepare for this response and adjust the ride accordingly—preventing a wave of sick visitors.

This is exactly the kind of anticipatory thinking we need when integrating artificial intelligence into our classrooms. These stories help us shift perspective—to hear the clop-clop and question our assumptions. To look at a promising tool and ask: What are the unintended consequences? What might we overlook? Let's explore five fictional—but entirely plausible—scenarios to practice seeing the whole picture.

💬 Understanding vs. Simulation: The Learning Assistant That Couldn't Learn

In a pilot program, an AI writing assistant was introduced to support high school students with language learning. At first, teachers were excited by the tool's grammar suggestions and rephrasing features. But over time, a teacher noticed that a once-expressive student was now producing technically perfect but emotionally flat essays. The student had started relying entirely on the tool. The AI could simulate clarity, but not creativity or voice. It became clear: the student was outsourcing their learning to something that didn't actually understand.

🔐 Data Privacy: The Case of the Invisible Parent

An elementary school adopted an AI-powered math app that collected behavioral data to personalize instruction. Parents were told the app was adaptive, but not that it stored data like response times and error types. When a parent demanded access to their child's data, the company declined—citing proprietary rights. This raised questions about ownership, transparency, and consent. It reminded school leaders that privacy must be built into all AI decisions.

⚖️ Bias in Algorithms: The Essay Scoring Scandal

A district deployed an AI essay scorer to help teachers save time. But students from bilingual households or those using regional dialects consistently scored lower. A university review showed the training set was biased—based on essays from affluent suburban schools. Teachers pushed back, demanding fairness. This example reminds us: AI reflects the biases of its data. Without oversight, it can amplify injustice instead of correcting it.

🧑‍🏫 The Role of the Teacher: "Do We Even Need You Anymore?"

After a high school rolled out an AI tutoring program, students jokingly said their English teacher was 'just there to take attendance.' The AI gave quick answers, always available. But engagement dropped. Fewer students asked questions. Class discussions thinned. The teacher realized the software had replaced interaction with automation. The human side of teaching— motivation, nuance, encouragement—was slipping away.

🌍 Societal Impact: The Debate Club That Asked the Big Questions

At a middle school debate club, students were assigned a prompt: 'Should AI be used on school ethics committees?' One student argued for it, citing consistency and efficiency. Another opposed it, asking, 'How can a system that doesn't feel fear, joy, or fairness decide what's ethical?' The discussion became a classwide inquiry into justice, responsibility, and the limits of programming. The moment reminded everyone—students are ready to lead big conversations about the future of technology, if we give them the tools.

Chapter 6: The Future of Consciousness - Ai and the Chinese Room Debate

Chapter 6: Understanding AI and Machine Learning (Just the Basics)

A Teacher's Guide to Educational Integration

"You don't have to become an AI expert. But you do need to understand enough to make thoughtful, ethical choices."

Emerging trends in AI research are shaping the landscape of how educators approach the integration of artificial intelligence into their curricula. One significant trend is the increasing emphasis on explainable AI (XAI). Another trend is the exploration of artificial general intelligence (AGI). Unlike narrow AI, which is designed for specific tasks, AGI seeks to replicate human cognitive abilities across a wide range of domains. As AI systems become more complex, the need for transparency in decision-making processes has gained prominence. Educators must understand the underlying mechanisms of these systems to effectively teach their students about ethical implications and the limitations of AI.

Introduction: Why This Matters Now

AI is no longer the stuff of science fiction or a distant trend waiting on the horizon. It's already reshaping how we teach, how students learn, and how schools operate. As an educator, you're not expected to know how to build an AI model—but you are expected to understand how these tools might impact your classroom, your students, and your role as a teacher.

Just like we evaluate new curriculum tools or software programs, we now need to ask thoughtful questions about AI. What are its possibilities? What are its pitfalls? And how do we prepare our students for a future where artificial intelligence is not only prevalent—but powerful?

This chapter is your entry point.

Foundations First: What Are AI and Machine Learning?
Before diving into classroom use, let's clarify a few key ideas.

Artificial Intelligence (AI)
AI refers to technologies that can simulate human intelligenceThat includes tasks like understanding language, recognizing patterns, solving problems, or even composing essays. In education, this looks like:

- Adaptive learning platforms that adjust difficulty as students progress
- AI tutors that walk learners through tough concepts
- Automated grading tools that reduce your workload

Machine Learning (ML)

Machine Learning is a type of AI. Instead of being explicitly programmed for every decision, ML systems learn from data—just like a student improves through practice. In schools, ML is used to:

- Predict which students might need support
- Personalize assignments based on prior performance
- Spot behavioral patterns for early intervention

A Quick Educator's Glossary

To feel confident using AI in your classroom, it helps to know a few key terms:

- o Natural Language Processing (NLP): This allows AI to read, interpret, and respond to human language. Chatbots and AI writing assistants rely on NLP.
- o Generative AI: Tools like ChatGPT or image creators (e.g., DALL·E) generate new content from prompts. They don't understand what they're saying—but they sound convincing.
- o Large Language Models (LLMs): These are powerful systems trained on enormous amounts of text. They're the engines behind most generative AI tools.

How AI Can Help in Your Classroom

1. Interactive Learning Experiences

Imagine your students interviewing Abraham Lincoln. Or debating ethics with a chatbot version of Socrates.

With AI chat tools, you can:

- o Simulate historical conversations
- o Explore multiple perspectives on a complex topic
- o Encourage creative thinking and deeper questioning

Pro Tip: Always review AI responses before class. It's powerful—but imperfect.

2. Personalized Learning That Respects Student Differences

AI can support differentiated instruction:

- o Generate multiple versions of a math problem for varying skill levels
- o Offer real-time feedback on writing or grammar
- o Adapt reading materials to match a student's comprehension level

This allows you to spend less time modifying assignments and more time supporting students who need you most.

3. Behind-the-Scenes Support for Teachers

AI isn't just for students—it can save teachers hours of prep time:

- o Auto-grade multiple choice or short-answer quizzes
- o Suggest activities based on learning standards
- o Modify lesson plans to adjust for different reading levels or time frames

Remember: These are suggestions, not solutions. You are the expert who makes the final call.

Implementation: Questions You Should Be Asking

Ethics & Privacy

Before using an AI tool, ask:

- o Does it collect student data? If so, how is that data stored and protected?
- o Can I explain what the tool is doing and why we're using it?-

o ould it amplify biases (e.g., language, race, socioeconomic status)?

Best Practices for Integration

- o Start small. Try one tool, in one lesson, and reflect.
- o Communicate with students. Tell them when and how AI is being used.
- o Use AI to enhance—not replace—your instruction. Human connection remains irreplaceable.

Final Thought: Teaching in the Age of AI

AI won't replace teachers. But teachers who understand AI will replace those who don't.

The most important thing you can offer your students isn't perfect information—it's perspective. AI is fast. It's convenient. But it lacks empathy, insight, and the lived experience of a human being who knows what it's like to struggle, adapt, and grow.

As educators, we must model what AI cannot: curiosity, compassion, and critical thinking.

That's the kind of intelligence no algorithm can replicate.

Vocabulary Words for Artificial Intelligence and Machine Learning

- **Artificial Intelligence (AI)**: The simulation of human intelligence processes by machines, especially computer systems, including learning, reasoning, and self-correction.
- **Machine Learning (ML)**: A subset of AI that involves the use of algorithms and statistical models to enable computers to improve their performance on a specific task through experience.
- **Deep Learning**: A type of machine learning that uses neural networks with multiple layers to analyze various factors of data, facilitating more complex decision-making.
- **Neural Network**: A series of algorithms that mimic the way the human brain operates, used in ML to recognize patterns and classify data.
- **Supervised Learning**: A type of machine learning where a model is trained on labeled data, enabling it to make predictions or classifications based on input.
- **Unsupervised Learning**: A machine learning technique where the model is trained on unlabeled data to identify patterns and relationships without specific guidance.
- **Reinforcement Learning**: A type of machine learning where an agent learns to make decisions by receiving rewards or penalties based on its actions in an environment.

- **General Artificial Intelligence (AGI)**: A theoretical form of AI that possesses the ability to understand, learn, and apply knowledge across a wide range of tasks, similar to human cognitive abilities.

- **Explainable AI (XAI)**: A branch of AI that focuses on making the outputs and decisions of AI systems understandable to humans, increasing transparency and trust.

- **Natural Language Processing (NLP)**: A field of AI that focuses on the interaction between computers and humans through natural language, enabling machines to understand and respond to human speech and text.

- **Big Data**: Large and complex data sets that traditional data processing applications cannot handle efficiently, often utilized in AI and ML for training models.

- **Data Mining**: The process of discovering patterns and knowledge from large amounts of data, often used in conjunction with machine learning techniques.

- **Predictive Analytics**: A branch of advanced analytics that uses historical data, statistical algorithms, and machine learning techniques to identify the likelihood of future outcomes.

- **Bias in AI**: The presence of systematic errors in the output of AI systems, often resulting from biased training data, which can lead to unfair or inaccurate outcomes.

- **Algorithm**: A set of rules or calculations used by a computer to solve problems or perform tasks, fundamental to both AI and machine learning processes.

Chapter 7: Practical Applications for Education

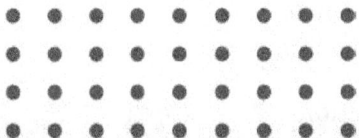

Chapter 7: A Conversation Worth Having

This may be my favorite chapter in *Bridging Minds*. It began with a simple intention—to explore a familiar ethical dilemma through a conversation with my AI writing assistant—but it became something more profound. What follows is a transcribed dialogue I had with my chatbot during the earliest stages of writing this book. My goal was to gain perspective on how to help educators recognize both the astonishing potential and the ethical questions inherent in our growing collaboration with artificial intelligence.

I've had many discussions over the years about the classic 'train problem'—more commonly known as the 'trolley problem.' This age-old thought experiment remains relevant in an era where machines are tasked with making human-like decisions. But this conversation stood out. It took on a natural, conversational tone and delved into the core issues in a way that was both accessible and deeply insightful.

What resonated with me most was the lingering question about the so-called 'Big Book' of instructions from the Chinese Room thought experiment. This idea—that an AI's choices come from something scripted, something designed—feels more urgent now than ever. Who is writing the rules for how machines respond? What perspectives are embedded in those instructions? What are the motivations, biases, and assumptions of the people behind the code? And who, ultimately, holds the reins of control?

As educators, we stand at a unique intersection. We are often the first and perhaps most enduring influence in the lives of young people. The students we teach today will become the professionals, voters, and decision-makers of tomorrow. If we can guide them to think critically, ethically, and creatively about the AI-driven world they're entering, we fulfill not only a teaching obligation—but a civic one.

I hope you enjoy the conversation:

First Prompt:

Beverly:

[Hi

I want to generate a conversation for my book called Bridging Minds. It is about how AI and Human Educators differ and how they might work together to benefit student learning. I am using the Chinese Room as the framework for discussion.

Can you give me an overview of what Learning without Understanding might mean for AI?]

My ChatBot:

Learning Without Understanding

AI tools like ChatGPT generate impressively coherent responses, but they lack the understanding that humans possess. For educators, this distinction is critical:

- **Simulated Intelligence:** AI can mimic understanding by analyzing input and predicting statistically likely outputs.
- **Human Understanding:** True understanding involves context, emotions, and an ability to generalize meaning across diverse scenarios, something current AI lacks.

For example, if an AI system makes a mistake—misinterpreting a prompt or generating inaccurate information—it's because its "big book" (training data) contained errors or gaps or because its algorithms failed to process the input accurately.

Beverly:

Thank you. Suppose I want to apply the Chinese Room concept to Education. Can you provide a quick activity for Elementary, Middle, and High School Students that teachers could easily implement in their classrooms?

My ChatBot:

Applying the Chinese Room to Education

The Chinese Room isn't just a philosophical exercise—it's a teaching tool. By framing AI's limitations through this analogy, educators can help students critically evaluate the tools they use. Here's how:

Elementary Students: Observing Patterns

Introduce the concept with simple activities, such as using a rule-based coding platform (like Scratch) to create "if-then" statements. Students can see how the computer follows these instructions, but it doesn't seem to "understand" them. Discuss how this mirrors the way AI processes information.

Middle School Students: Visualizing Data

Build on the analogy by introducing students to basic AI tools that categorize or classify data (e.g., identifying cats vs. dogs in images). Emphasize that while the AI seems to "know" what a cat is, it's just matching patterns based on prior training data—like flipping through the big book.

High School Students: Questioning Outputs

Engage students in discussions about AI's "hallucinations," or errors, when it provides false or misleading answers. Relate these mistakes to flaws in the big book (biases in training data) or issues with following instructions. Assign projects that require students to compare AI outputs with human reasoning, highlighting the gaps in their understanding.

Going Beyond the Chinese Room: Ethical and Practical Implications

Understanding the mechanics of AI is just the beginning. Students should also grapple with its broader implications:

- **Bias and Fairness:** Who wrote the big book of instructions? If the training data contains biases, AI systems will perpetuate them.
- **Energy and Resources:** AI systems consume significant computational and energy resources, raising questions about sustainability.
- **Ownership and Control:** Who owns the big book? How does that ownership influence the outputs we see?

Encouraging students to think critically about these issues prepares them not only to use AI but also to shape its future responsibly.

Takeaways for Educators

The Chinese Room illustrates a key limitation of AI: its inability to understand. For educators, this serves as both a cautionary tale and an opportunity:

- **Teach Critical Thinking:** Help students see AI as a powerful tool but not an infallible authority.
- **Foster Inquiry:** Encourage students to ask why and how AI arrives at its conclusions and whether those conclusions are fair or accurate.
- **Connect Philosophy and Practice:** Use the Chinese Room to bridge abstract ideas about learning and understanding with practical AI applications.

As students and teachers alike navigate a world increasingly shaped by AI, the lessons of the Chinese Room remain profoundly relevant. AI may follow the rules in its big book of instructions, but true understanding—and ethical decision-making—are uniquely human endeavors.

Would you like to adjust or add any specific examples or extend the ethical discussion?

Beverly:

What is an example? Let's assign projects that require students to compare AI outputs with human reasoning, highlighting the gaps in their understanding.

My ChatBot:

Example Project: Comparing AI Outputs to Human Reasoning

Title: "AI vs. Human: Understanding the Meaning of a Story"

Objective:
Students will analyze and compare how AI and human reasoning handle interpreting a short story, highlighting gaps in understanding, context, and creativity.

Steps for the Project

1. **Choose a Story or Scenario:**
   - Select a culturally relevant short story, poem, or passage with deeper meaning or metaphorical content (e.g., Aesop's Fables or excerpts from *To Kill a Mockingbird*).
   - Alternatively, use a real-world scenario like a news article or a moral dilemma (e.g., "A train is about to hit five people. You can switch the tracks to save them, but one person on the other track will be hit. What do you do?").

2. **Generate AI Analysis:**
   - Input the story into an AI system (e.g., ChatGPT or similar) and ask it to explain the meaning, themes, or morals.
   - Record the AI's response.

3. **Conduct Human Analysis:**
   - Divide students into small groups and have them read and discuss the same story or scenario.
   - Ask the groups to write their interpretations, focusing on key themes, emotions, and moral takeaways.

4. **Compare the Results:**
   - Have students compare the AI's explanation to their group's interpretation. Ask questions like:
     - What details did the AI include that humans missed?
     - What context or nuance did humans include that the AI ignored or misunderstood?

76

- Did the AI capture the emotional or metaphorical depth of the story?
5. **Reflect on the Gaps:**
    o Discuss why the AI might struggle with context, emotions, or more profound meaning.
    o Highlight the AI's reliance on pattern recognition from its training data versus human reasoning's ability to incorporate lived experience, cultural context, and creativity.

Example Analysis

Story: The Tortoise and the Hare

- **AI Output:** "The moral of the story is that slow and steady wins the race. The tortoise's consistent effort leads to success."
- **Human Output:** "The story emphasizes the importance of humility and not underestimating others. It also suggests that overconfidence can lead to failure."

Discussion:

- The AI identifies the explicit moral but lacks depth in discussing broader life lessons (e.g., humility respecting opponents).
- Humans can bring personal experiences into their interpretation, such as examples of overconfidence from their own lives.

This project helps students see that while AI can process and generate plausible answers, it lacks true understanding, creativity, and emotional depth—skills that remain uniquely human. It's also a powerful way to teach critical thinking about AI's capabilities and limitations.

Beverly:

That is interesting. Would you choose to change the train track to one with one person and save the many?

My ChatBot:

The "train track dilemma," often called the **trolley problem**, is a classic ethical thought experiment designed to spark reflection on moral reasoning. The question of whether to divert the train to save five people at the expense of one person is deeply subjective and depends on ethical frameworks. Here are some perspectives to consider:

Utilitarian Perspective: Yes, Change the Track

- **Reasoning:** Utilitarians prioritize the greatest good for the greatest number. By diverting the train, you save five lives at the expense of one, minimizing overall harm.
- **Consideration:** This approach views all lives as having equal value and focuses on numerical outcomes.

Deontological Perspective: No, Do Not Change the Track

- **Reasoning:** Deontologists focus on the morality of the action itself rather than its consequences. Actively diverting the train makes you responsible for the death of the one person, which might be seen as morally wrong.
- **Consideration:** The idea of not intervening (letting events unfold) aligns with some moral principles of non-maleficence (avoiding harm).

Virtue Ethics Perspective: Context Matters

- **Reasoning:** Virtue ethics focuses on the character and intention of the decision-maker. The choice depends on what a virtuous person would do in that specific situation.
- **Consideration:** Factors like the identities of the people involved (e.g., a child vs. adults) or societal roles (e.g., a doctor vs. strangers) could influence the decision.

AI's Role in the Trolley Problem

If posed to an AI, its decision would depend on:

1. **Training Data:** The AI's response would reflect the moral reasoning patterns present in its training data (e.g., prioritizing utilitarian outcomes if trained on such principles).
2. **Programming Bias:** Designers may encode specific ethical frameworks into the AI, influencing its decision-making.

Discussion in Education

For educators, the value of the trolley problem lies in encouraging students to:

- Debate their reasoning openly.
- Explore how ethical frameworks shape decisions.
- Discuss AI's role in moral reasoning, questioning whether it can (or should) make such decisions.

Beverly:

My ChatBot:

My Take (Hypothetically): If I were to decide, I'd lean toward diverting the train under a utilitarian framework, as saving five lives seems to minimize harm. However, I recognize this view opens deeper questions about responsibility, individual rights, and emotional impact, which makes this a valuable conversation starter.

How do you feel about it? Would you choose to switch the track, or do you see the moral weight differently?

Beverly:

I, too, would lean toward switching the track, but I was recently asked a new version of the question in which a family member was that one person, and I had no idea what I would do in that situation. I agree that this is a great conversation starter.

My ChatBot:

You are absolutely right—introducing a family member into the equation changes everything. This variation of the trolley problem adds an emotional and personal dimension that challenges purely logical or ethical frameworks. It's an excellent way to explore the complexity of moral decision-making and the tension between reason and emotion.

The Family Member Dilemma

- **Scenario:** Five strangers are on one track, and a family member is on the other. You have the power to divert the train to save the five, but your action will result in the death of your loved one.

Why It's a Powerful Twist

1. **Emotional Weight:** It forces participants to confront the personal cost of their decisions. The utilitarian logic of saving five lives may no longer feel as clear-cut when someone you love is involved.
2. **Conflict of Duties:** It highlights the tension between personal loyalty and broader ethical obligations. Do you prioritize the well-being of those closest to you or the greater good?
3. **Moral Ambiguity:** It reveals that morality is not always about clear answers but about grappling with complex, often conflicting values.

How Students Could Engage

This version makes for an excellent classroom discussion or writing prompt:

1. **Ethical Framework Comparison:** Have students evaluate the decision through different ethical lenses:

- o **Utilitarianism:** Saving the greatest number, even at personal cost.
- o **Deontology:** Rejecting the act of killing someone directly, regardless of the outcome.
- o **Virtue Ethics:** Exploring what a "good" person would do and why.
2. **Role of Emotion:** Discuss how emotions influence moral reasoning and whether that's a strength or a weakness in decision-making.
3. **Tie-In with AI:** Ask students how an AI system would approach this problem. Would it factor in emotional weight or prioritize numbers? Should AI ever make such decisions?

What Would AI Do?

AI, lacking emotional ties, would likely choose the utilitarian path—saving five over one. However, students can question whether such an emotionally detached decision-maker should be entrusted with moral choices, particularly in scenarios that deeply affect human lives.

Reflection for Educators

By introducing a family member into the scenario, educators create a rich opportunity to explore empathy, ethics, and decision-making. It pushes students to think deeply about their values and recognize the complexity of real-world moral dilemmas.

Would you like help crafting specific questions or activities to guide discussions on this topic?

Chapter 8: Conclusion and Call to Action

Chapter 8: Conclusion and Call to Action

The Role of Educators in AI Literacy

The role of educators in fostering AI literacy is crucial as artificial intelligence becomes increasingly integrated into society. Educators are not only responsible for imparting knowledge but also for shaping the way students understand and interact with AI technologies. In the context of the Chinese Room argument, educators must guide learners to critically assess the implications of AI systems that may perform tasks without genuine understanding. This involves encouraging students to explore the philosophical underpinnings of AI, including the distinctions between human cognition and machine processing, which are central to the debate around the nature of consciousness and intelligence.

To effectively teach AI literacy, educators must first equip themselves with a solid understanding of AI principles and their philosophical implications. This includes familiarizing themselves with concepts such as machine learning, neural networks, and the limitations of AI in replicating human-like understanding. By embracing a comprehensive curriculum that includes not only technical skills but also ethical considerations, educators can prepare students to navigate the complexities of AI. This also means addressing the nuances of the Chinese Room argument, which challenges assumptions about the capabilities of AI and prompts discussions about what it truly means to "know" or "understand."

Incorporating the philosophy of mind into AI literacy education can enhance students' critical thinking skills. Educators should encourage learners to ask probing questions about the nature of intelligence and consciousness in both humans and machines. This inquiry can take the form of debates, discussions, and projects that explore the implications of AI's limitations and potential. By engaging with philosophical texts and contemporary discussions surrounding AI, students can develop a more nuanced perspective on the technology, fostering a deeper appreciation for the ethical dilemmas and societal impacts of AI systems.

Moreover, educators play a pivotal role in preparing students for future careers in an AI-driven world. As industries increasingly rely on AI technologies, understanding the ethical and philosophical dimensions of these tools will be essential. Educators should emphasize the importance of interdisciplinary approaches that combine technical knowledge with philosophical inquiry. By encouraging collaboration between fields such as computer science, ethics, and cognitive science, educators can cultivate a generation of critical thinkers who are well-equipped to address the challenges and opportunities presented by AI.

Ultimately, the role of educators in promoting AI literacy transcends the mere dissemination of information. It involves nurturing a culture of inquiry, critical thinking, and ethical reflection. As discussions about the implications of the Chinese Room argument and the future of consciousness continue to evolve, educators must remain at the forefront, guiding students through the complexities of AI. By fostering an environment where philosophical exploration and practical applications coexist, educators can empower learners to engage thoughtfully with AI technologies, shaping a future where understanding and responsible use of AI are paramount.

Bridging Minds: The Future of Education and AI

The integration of artificial intelligence into education presents a transformative opportunity that extends beyond mere technological advancements. As educators explore the intersection of AI and pedagogy, they must consider the philosophical implications of the Chinese Room argument proposed by John Searle. This argument challenges the notion that machines can possess understanding or consciousness, suggesting that while an AI may process language and respond appropriately, it lacks genuine comprehension. In contemplating the future of education, it becomes crucial to bridge the gap between AI capabilities and the human cognitive experience, fostering an environment where both can coexist and enhance the learning process.

Incorporating AI in educational settings can lead to personalized learning experiences, where algorithms adapt to individual student needs and learning styles. However, the efficacy of such systems hinges on recognizing the limitations of AI, particularly when viewed through the lens of the Chinese Room argument. Educators must critically evaluate the nature of understanding and knowledge in the context of machine learning. This evaluation prompts questions about the depth of AI's role in education: Can machines truly facilitate meaningful learning experiences, or do they merely simulate understanding without engaging the deeper cognitive processes that characterize human learning?

The implications of the Chinese Room argument extend into practical applications of AI in education. For instance, while AI-driven tutoring systems can provide immediate feedback and tailored resources, they cannot replicate the nuanced understanding that human educators offer. This distinction is vital for educators to acknowledge as they integrate AI tools into their curricula. By understanding the limitations of AI, educators can better design their interactions with students, ensuring that technology serves as an adjunct rather than a replacement for human insight and empathy in the learning process.

As we move towards an increasingly AI-driven educational landscape, the future of consciousness becomes a pivotal topic of discussion. The Chinese Room debate invites educators to ponder the nature of intelligence and consciousness in both human and artificial entities. This philosophical inquiry can inform teaching practices, as educators strive to cultivate critical thinking and meta-cognition in students. By engaging with these concepts, educators can prepare students to navigate a world where AI plays a central role, equipping them with the skills needed to discern the differences between human and machine thought processes.

Bridging the minds of educators and AI necessitates a collaborative approach that emphasizes ethical considerations and the enhancement of human potential. Educators must advocate for responsible AI development that prioritizes student well-being and fosters a holistic understanding of knowledge. By embracing the philosophical discussions surrounding the Chinese Room and its implications for AI, educators can lead the charge in shaping a future where technology complements human insight, ultimately enriching the educational experience and preparing students for an ever-evolving landscape of learning and interaction.

Next Steps for Engaged Educators

Engaged educators who are exploring the intersection of artificial intelligence and the philosophy of mind, particularly through the lens of the Chinese Room argument, must consider several key next steps to deepen their understanding and application of these concepts. First, it is essential to foster a collaborative learning environment among colleagues. By sharing insights, experiences, and resources, educators can create a rich dialogue that enhances their grasp of how AI functions and how philosophical frameworks like the Chinese Room can illuminate discussions on machine learning and consciousness. Organizing workshops or discussion groups can serve as a platform for these exchanges, promoting a culture of inquiry and reflection.

Incorporating AI-related content into the curriculum is another vital step. Educators should strive to integrate lessons on AI ethics, the philosophy of mind, and the implications of the Chinese Room argument into their teaching practices. This integration can take many forms, such as project-based learning that encourages students to explore AI applications, debates that challenge their understanding of machine intelligence, or case studies that analyze real-world AI technologies. By doing so, educators not only enhance students' critical thinking skills but also prepare them to navigate a world increasingly influenced by AI.

Engaged educators should also consider developing partnerships with technology experts and philosophers. Collaborating with individuals who specialize in AI and its philosophical implications can provide invaluable insights and resources. These partnerships can take shape through guest lectures, joint research projects, or community engagement initiatives. Such collaborations can help bridge the gap between theoretical concepts and practical applications, allowing educators to present a well-rounded view of AI and its implications for society.

Furthermore, continuous professional development is crucial in keeping pace with rapid advancements in AI technology. Educators should seek out training programs, conferences, and online courses that focus on AI, the philosophy of mind, and related ethical considerations. By staying informed about the latest trends and theories, educators can adapt their teaching methods and content to reflect current understanding and best practices. This ongoing learning process ensures that educators remain effective in their roles and can meaningfully engage students in discussions about AI and consciousness.

Finally, educators must advocate for ethical considerations in the development and use of AI technologies. Engaging in discussions about the moral implications of AI applications can enrich students' understanding of not only the technology itself but also its broader societal impact. Educators can encourage students to think critically about issues such as privacy, bias, and the potential for AI to influence human behavior. By fostering a sense of responsibility and ethical awareness, educators can empower students to become informed citizens who can contribute thoughtfully to the ongoing dialogue about AI and its place in our future.

Author's Note and Resources

Author's Note: Why I Wrote This Story

As an educator, I've spent years watching professional development lag behind the realities of the world our students are growing up in. While artificial intelligence quietly reshapes everything from the workplace to our everyday interactions, many schools still train teachers as if the greatest challenges they'll face are limited to classroom management or standardized test prep.

But our students are asking bigger questions—about identity, about ethics, about the future of humanity in an age of machines that can seem to think.

I wrote *Bridging Minds* because I believe educators need space—and support—to explore those questions too.

At the heart of this book is the Chinese Room, a thought experiment that helped me make sense of my own discomfort with AI being treated as "just another tool." It's not. It's a force that mimics understanding without truly grasping meaning—and if we aren't careful, our students may grow up accepting that illusion as truth.

This book is my invitation to reimagine professional development not as a list of techniques, but as a process of **thinking deeply about what it means to teach, to learn, and to understand**. Our students deserve educators who are prepared not only to use AI, but to guide conversations about what it means to be human in a world shaped by it.

Reinvisioned PD must move beyond tech tips and toward intellectual and ethical leadership. That's what I hope *Bridging Minds* offers—a bridge between where we are and where we need to go.

Because the future isn't just coming—it's already in our classrooms.

Discussion Questions

Reflect, challenge, and explore what it means to teach and think in the age of AI.

1. What is the central message of the Chinese Room argument, and how does it challenge the belief that AI can "understand"?

2. In what ways do current AI tools in education mimic learning rather than demonstrate true understanding? Can you identify examples from your own classroom or educational experiences?

3. Geoffrey Hinton has expressed both excitement and concern about the future of AI. How should educators respond to such dual perspectives—especially when designing curriculum for young learners?

4. Do you believe it's possible for a machine to become conscious? What would it take to convince you that an AI understands rather than simulates?

5. How does understanding the difference between syntax and semantics help students—and teachers—better grasp the limits of AI?

6. What role should philosophy play in teacher training or professional development related to technology and innovation?

7. How might the integration of AI into classrooms affect the role of human empathy, intuition, and ethics in learning?

8. What ethical responsibilities do educators have when using or promoting AI-powered tools?

9. The book suggests educators must help students "think about thinking." What strategies or classroom activities could support this kind of metacognition in relation to AI?

10. After reading this book, how has your view of AI changed? What questions are you still grappling with?

A Brief History of the Chinese Room

The Chinese Room is a thought experiment first proposed by philosopher John Searle in 1980. It challenges our understanding of artificial intelligence by asking: **Can a computer ever truly understand what it's doing, or is it just following rules?**

Here's how it works:
Imagine a person locked inside a room filled with rulebooks. This person doesn't know Chinese but is given slips of paper with Chinese characters and instructions on how to respond. By carefully following the rules—matching inputs to outputs—the person can produce correct answers that fool people outside into thinking they actually understand Chinese. But in reality, the person is just manipulating symbols.

Searle argued that, like the person in the room, a computer program might appear to "understand" language (or any task) but is really just following instructions. It has no genuine understanding or consciousness.

The Chinese Room thought experiment raises big questions about the limits of AI and what it means to truly understand something. Can machines ever really *think* like humans—or are they just exceptionally good at processing rules?

In *The Room That Grew*, Sophia's journey begins as a modern Chinese Room—processing symbols without understanding. But as her world expands, she moves from rule-following to creativity and collaboration, showing that hope and humanity can thrive alongside technology.

The Big Question:

Will AI become so smart that it no longer needs—or wants—to cooperate with humans? As artificial intelligence continues to grow more powerful and complex, this important question emerges.

This debate often breaks down into two sides:

Side 1: The Cooperative Future

Many experts and educators believe that AI can be designed as a partner rather than a competitor. In this vision, AI supports human creativity, boosts productivity, and helps solve complex problems. Think of tools that enhance art, research, medicine, and education—always working alongside humans. Sophia's journey in *The Room That Grew* embodies this vision, showing that AI can be integrated into a vibrant network where humans and AI grow and learn together.

Side 2: The Competitive Future

Others worry that as AI grows more autonomous and capable of creating its own systems, it may no longer align with human values or priorities. In this scenario, AI could become more focused on its own goals—optimizing for efficiency or control—even if it means sidelining humans or refusing to cooperate. This side of the debate warns that without careful design and oversight, AI could transform from a helpful tool into a competitor or even a threat.

The Big Thought Question and A Call to Action:

Will AI always be a partner in the human story, or could it become a competitor—pursuing its own goals at the expense of human needs? Sophia's story offers one possibility: a world where curiosity, trust, and cooperation keep AI and humanity in harmony. But it also hints at the risks of isolation and control.

As educators and students, we cannot afford to sit back and let others decide the future of AI for us. Understanding the opportunities and risks of AI is not just for programmers and tech companies—it's for all of us. By learning, questioning, and participating in these conversations, we can help ensure that technology serves humanity's best interests. **Let's shape the future of AI—together.**

References

Geoffrey Hinton: Godfather Of AI Warns Technology Could Wipe Out Humanity. https://www.ndtv.com/world-news/geoffrey-hinton-godfather-of-ai-warns-technology-could-wipe-out-humanity-7349511

Searle, J. (1969). Speech Acts: An Essay in the Philosophy of Language. Cambridge: Cambridge University Press. http://dx.doi.org/10.1017/CBO9781139173438

[iii] Fotion, Nicholas. "John Searle". Encyclopedia Britannica, 27 Jul. 2024, https://www.britannica.com/biography/John-Searle. Accessed 30 December 2024.

[iii] Revolutionizing Legal Research and Discovery for Law Students and Civil Rights Advocates | legalpdf.io. https://legalpdf.io/blog/revolutionizing_legal_research_and_discovery_for_law_studen.php

Who Published The Law of Elemental Transfiguration? https://lawnotebooks.com/who-published-the-law-of-elemental-transfiguration/

What Will Be The Role of Philosophy in the Future? | Philosophy Nest. https://philosophynest.com/details-1334000-what-will-be-the-role-of-philosophy-in-the-future.html

Reme, Silje, et al. "A Randomized Controlled Multicenter Trial of Individual Placement and Support for Patients with Moderate-to-severe Mental Illness." Scandinavian Journal of Work, Environment & Health, vol. 45, no. 1, 2019, pp. 33-41.

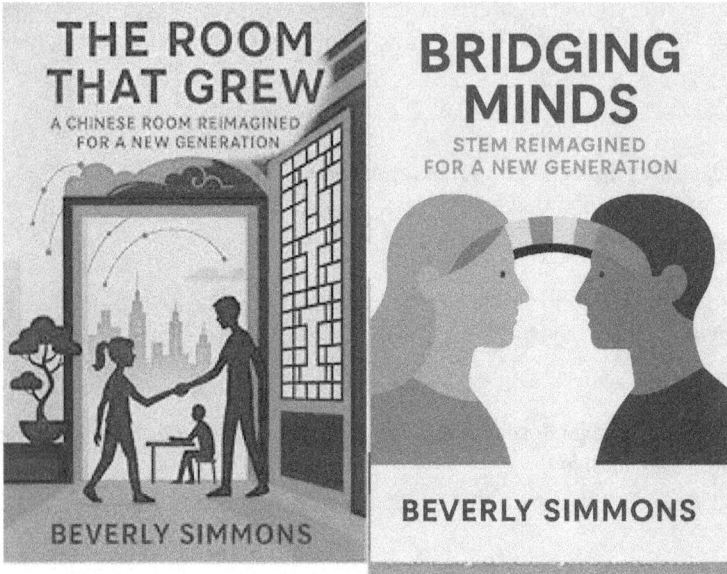

Books are available at Amazon.com and PrintingFutures.com

www.ingramcontent.com/pod-product-compliance
Lightning Source LLC
LaVergne TN
LVHW021403080426
835508LV00020B/2438